A TALE OF "O"

Also by Rosabeth Moss Kanter

Commitment and Community (1972)
Communes: Creating and Managing the Collective Life, editor (1973)
Another Voice, edited with Marcia Millman (1975)
Work and Family in the United States (1977)
Men and Women of the Corporation (1977)
Life in Organizations, edited with Barry A. Stein (1979)

♦ HARPER TORCHBOOKS
▼ Harper & Row, Publishers, New York

Cambridge, Philadelphia, San Francisco
London, Mexico City, São Paulo, Singapore, Sydney

A Tale of "O"

On Being Different in an Organization

**Rosabeth Moss Kanter
with Barry A. Stein**

illustrated by
Booth Simpson Designers

Portions of this work originally appeared in *Ms.* magazine.

First HARPER TORCHBOOKS edition published 1986.

Library of Congress Cataloging in Publication Data

Kanter, Rosabeth Moss
  A tale of "O".

  "Harper Torchbooks."
  1. Organizational behavior. 2. Conformity.
  3. Discrimination in employment. I. Stein, Barry,
  HD58.7.K37 1986   658.3'145   79-2625
  ISBN 0-06-132064-1 (pbk.)

89   90   10   9   8   7   6   5   4

A TALE OF "O"

This is a familiar drama performed every day in every place where there are many more of some kinds of people than of others—where some people have an easy time fitting in because they're just like everyone else, while other people have problems because . . . they are different.

There are two kinds of characters in this story:

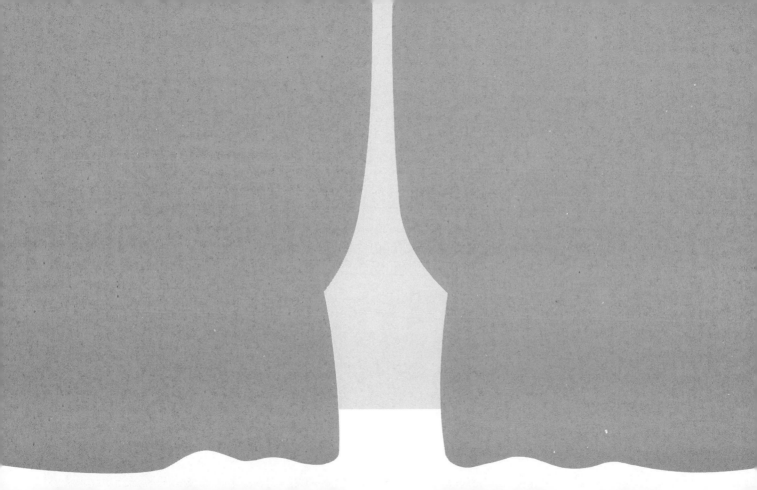

The X's—

the people who are found in large numbers—

and the O's—

the people who are scarce.

O

O

O

The X's and the O's could be anybody.

What makes people X's or O's is just how common
they are in a particular place. From then on, they play a role
that may have little to do with what they are really like as
people. The O's seem "different" just because there are so few
of them compared to the X's.

If you've ever felt different from the people around you, for
any reason—sex, race, age, size, religion, language, job or
technical specialty—you'll know what we mean.

Let's take a look at a typical work group in an organization—
composed of seven X's and one O—and see what's going on.

What happens to the only O in a group of X's?

X X O X X X X X X

The first thing we notice is that the O stands out, the O is eye-catching, the O gets more of our awareness and attention than any one of the X's. We put a spotlight on the O. Watch what happens as the members of the group move around.

The Spotlight

X
X
O
X
X
X
X
X

As they move, it's the O we follow with our eyes.
We notice where the O is, but we pay much less attention
to the different X's.

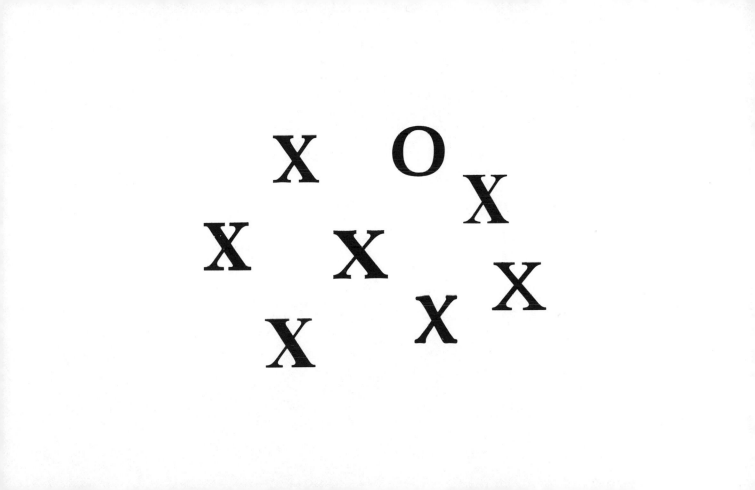

The O's uniqueness gets it X-tra attention. We're distracted by the O; the O gets stared at—it's a novelty.

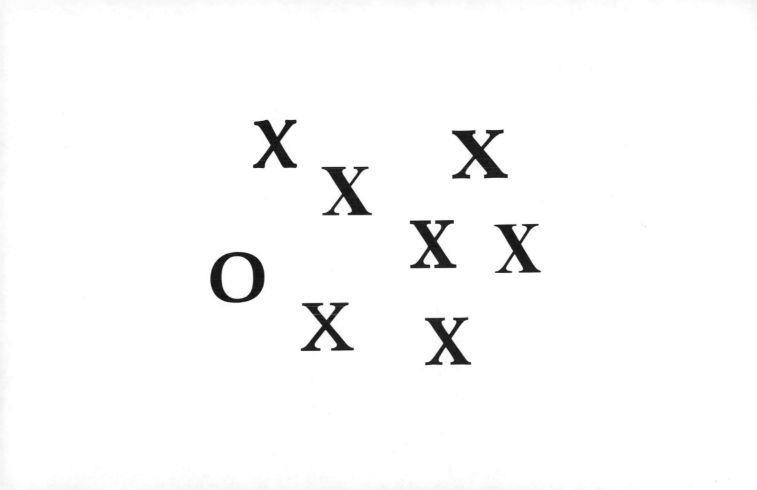

People will remember more about the O than about any one of the X's.

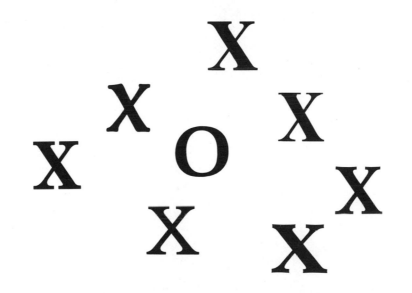

There will be more gossip about the O,

more stories and rumors about the O.

"Did you hear what happened in Dallas?"
"I heard they gave that sales job to an O."
"No kidding! What's gonna happen next?"
"I don't know, but I sure hope I don't have to work for one."

The O is always performing in the spotlight. Everything the O does is subject to public scrutiny. The O cannot hide its mistakes as easily as the X's can. And people make sure the O knows it.

"You are our test O. We're watching you to see how O's can handle this job. If you do well, we might get more O's."

"We've never had anyone like you in this department before, and we're all dying to know how it will work out."

28

This scrutiny can make the O feel that it's walking a tightrope. Even the smallest mistake could be fatal.

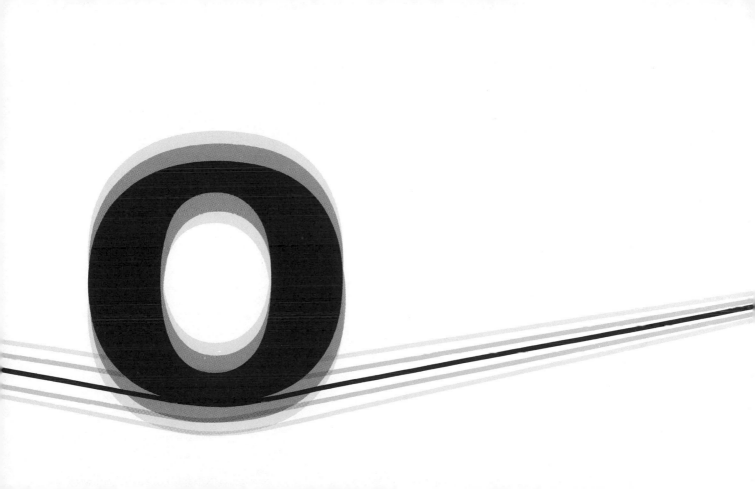

Sometimes the X's envy the O's for the special attention and publicity they get. After all, X's want to be noticed too, and it might not seem fair. But the O's greater visibility is not the kind that brings power and advancement, because what we're noticing is not the O's competence . . .

o

but its O-ness—whatever it is that makes the O different.

That's what we see first when we see an O: how odd it is! Sometimes people don't hear a word the O says. They're too busy just staring at it. (That's why O-ness is a burden.)

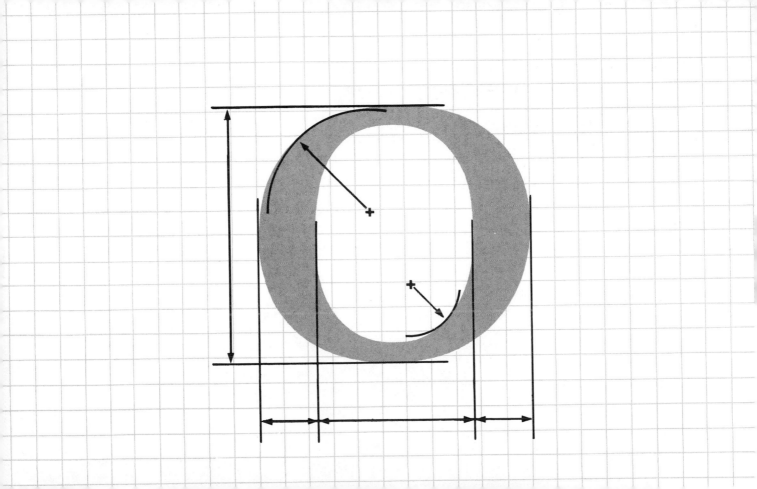

Thus O's often have to live up to two (sometimes conflicting) standards: first, whether they can demonstrate the same X-pertise as the X's, and . . .

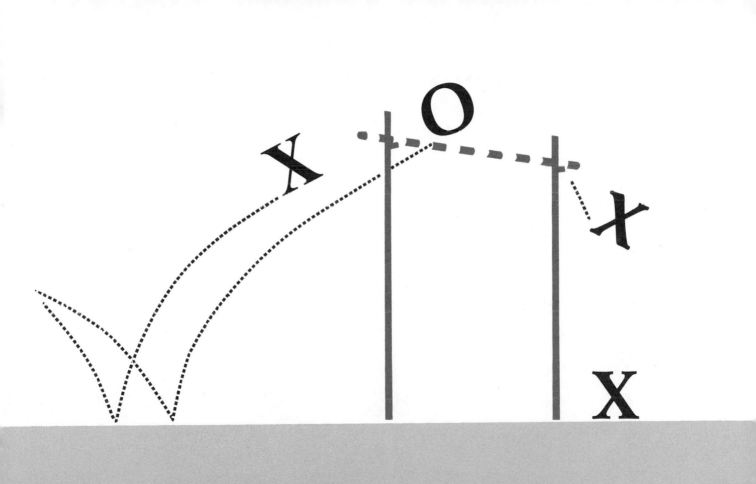

second, how well they live up to the X's idea of a "good O."

Being the Only or representative O also gives the O an X-tra job to do: serving as spokesO—talking for all O's. The O might be sent off to public events as a show O.

The O will be turned to in meetings and asked, *"What do you O's think about this?"*

The O will be asked to join committees to *"give us the O's point of view."* Or *"to speak at our next program; we're devoting it entirely to the problems of O's."*

Eventually, if the O does well, it will be X-pected to meet with every Board or Task Force or Planning group,

X O X X
X X X X
X

X
X
X X
X X
X X

X X X
X X X X

because they all need to include an O and . . .

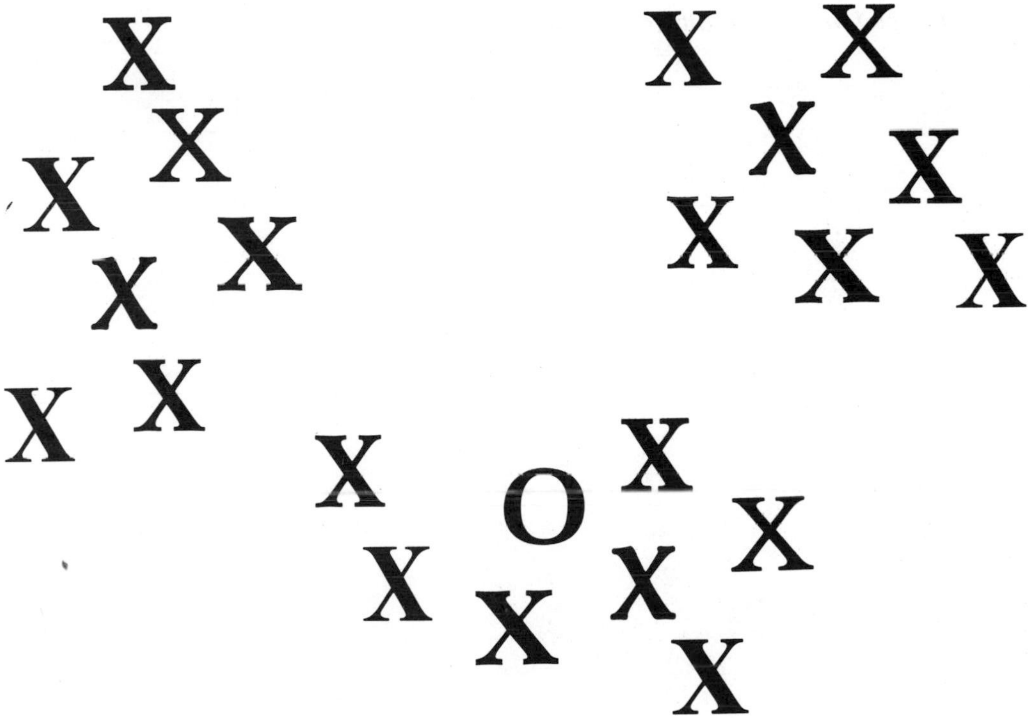

there seem to be *"so few other qualified O's around."*

X
X
X
X
X
X
X
X
X

X X O X
X X X
X X
X

X X X X
X X
X X X

For the O,
this often results in Overload.

(And then the X's wonder why *"O's can't take the heat."*)

How can the O cope with these performance pressures?

- The glare of the spotlight.
- Being noticed for the wrong things.
- Being X-pected to live up to two standards.
- Having to do its own job and also to serve as token O.

O's have tended to make one of three choices.

The first is:

O-verachievement.

Doing more, better and faster than any X.

Becoming a superstar O.

This is how a few very talented O's have always been able to succeed among the X's.

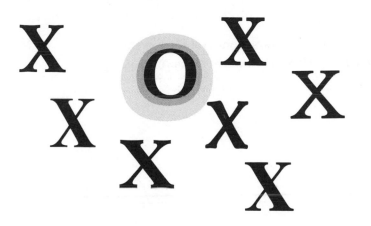

But not all O's can be superstars, just as not all X's are geniuses. So it's not fair for organizations to insist that all their O's be O-verachievers, when most of their X's are just average.

And some O's who could be superstars wonder if it's worth it: *"Why should I have to work harder than everybody else, just to keep my job?"*

We will know there is progress for O's when sO-sO O's get the same chance as un-X-traordinary X's.

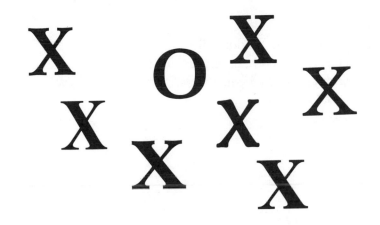

Some O's make a second choice: They try to look like an X, to blend into the crowd and become less visible by wearing X clothing, using X mannerisms and X language, or acting like an X.

But this can also create problems: the X's don't always X-ccept this. They ask: *"Why are you O's always trying to hide your O-ness? Why can't you just be yourselves?"*

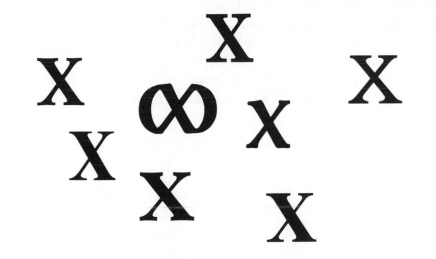

So some O's make a third choice: They avoid the competition altogether and step out of the spotlight, by hiding behind an X or taking a job behind the scenes. This relieves the stress of performing under constant pressure. The O can be just an assistant—the person who writes the report but doesn't deliver it in public. Some O's have always settled for helping someone else advance; for vicarious achievement through pushing someone else's career. You know what they say: *"Behind every great X is an O."*

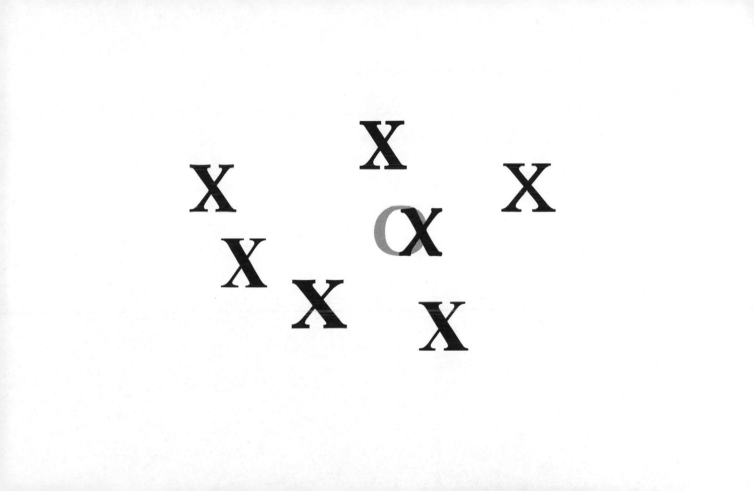

This last choice, dropping out, has led to a popular conclusion: *"O's fear success."*

But you can see that if O's fear *anything*, it is not success but too much visibility—the X-tra performance pressures that come with being the Only.

The second set of issues for O's concerns their relations to the X group.

The X Group

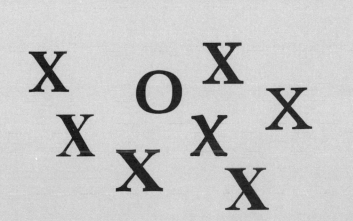

If a group is made up of all X's, we are much more likely
to notice the differences among them—the fact that each is a
distinct individual—than we are when we're busy watching
an O.

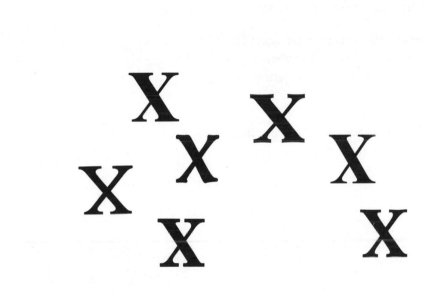

In fact, when there is an O, it makes the X's *more* of a group.

Suddenly they look more alike, seem more together than they otherwise would. The difference between any X and the O is so great that it O-verwhelms the differences among the X's.

It is a contrast effect. The presence of one thing that is different makes the others a category by contrast.

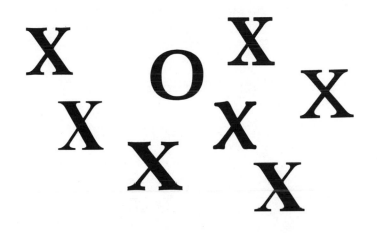

Actually, the X's never knew they had so much in
common . . .

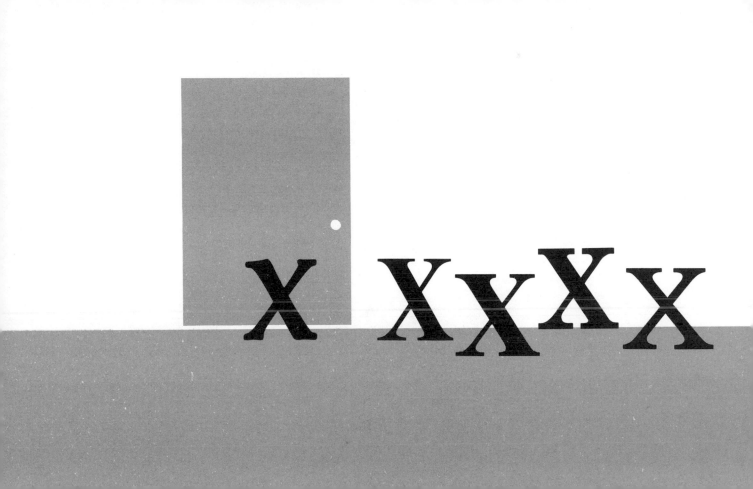

until the O walked into the room.

X's all these years have not been going around saying, *"We're the X's around here."* They were just *people* doing their jobs. But when an O comes, they suddenly remember that they are also X's.

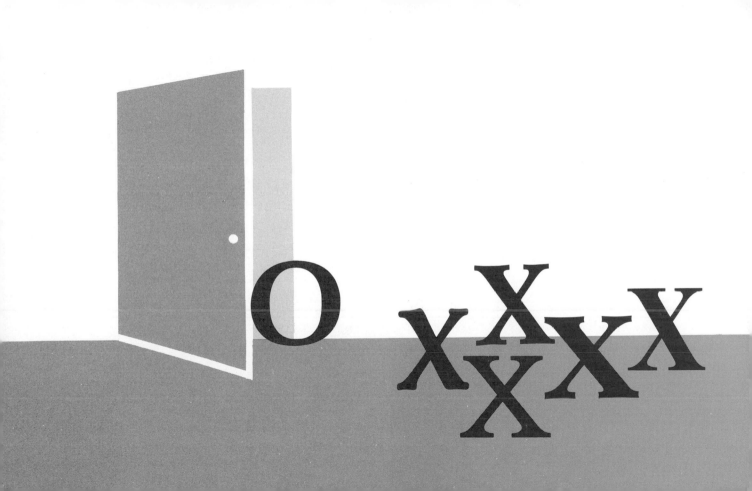

This X-tra awareness of X-ness can make the X's uncomfortable, like looking into a mirror for the first time. In fact, some of what seems like prejudice against O's is really just the X's discomfort at having to be more self-aware, at having to think about things that used to be natural.

For example, who wants to spend a lot of time figuring out how to get in and out of a crowded elevator?

Or worrying about whether the lunch menu will be suitable for O's? Or wondering what to talk about with those different people?

So the X's aren't sure things will ever be the same, now that the O is around.

"What about the things we like that O's aren't interested in?"

"I certainly hope we won't have to translate everything we say. That would really slow us down."

"Can we still have our meetings at the same place? I don't think O's go there."

"Can we still tell the same old stories?"

"Boy, things sure were easier in the old days."

The O, of course, has to honor the X's traditions. What one person would—or could—stop seven others from doing what they just said they always do? But the O is put on notice:

"You O's don't do those things."

"You O's don't belong."

These things help the X's remind each other that they are still X's and that the entry of an O hasn't changed anything. They need to make sure no one thinks they have lost their X-ness, and especially the O. So they X-aggerate their displays of X culture when the O is around.

Whatever it is that X's think O's think X's talk about, they're likely to talk about louder and more often in the presence of the O than they might if they were alone.

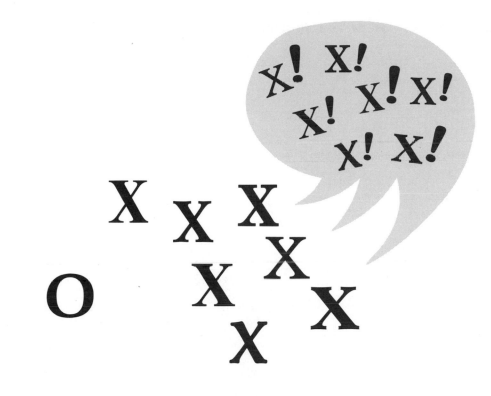

In this way, the X's close ranks against the O,

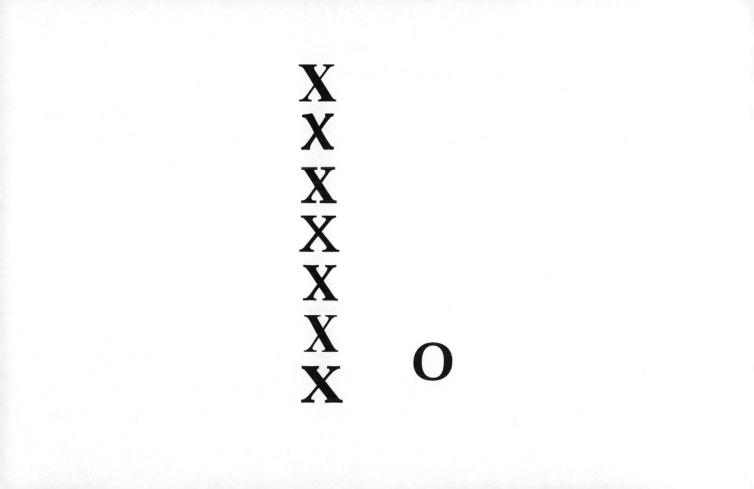

reminding the O that it is different, and is not X-pected to do or say the things the X's do.

O

The O gets pushed further to the sidelines, where it has to watch the action without joining it.

After all, there are *some* things X's think they should do by themselves. Anyway, *"X's will be X's."*

X
X
X
X
X
X

O

Sometimes X's interrupt a meeting when they use a word insulting to O's or that O's aren't "supposed" to use— or at least aren't supposed to understand.

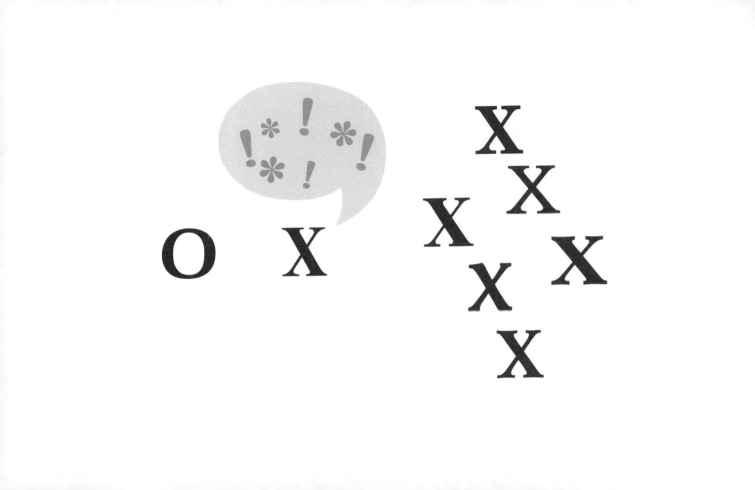

They apologize elaborately before going on. Of course, that simply draws *more* attention to the O as someone different.

The X's may think they're just being polite, but it puts the O on the spot anyway.

Now, the O might use "that word" all the time (at home, on weekends, with friends): it might be one of the O's favorite X-pressions.

But it has now been warned that it had better not say it around the X's because the X's won't accept it from an O. That would make the O look un-O-like.

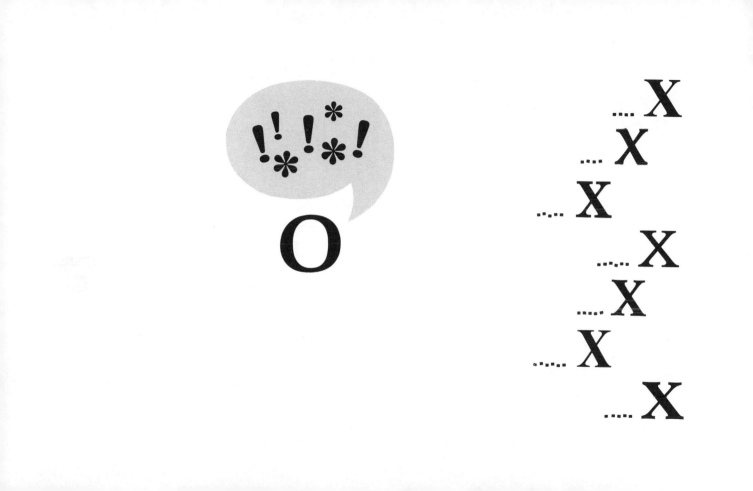

So instead the O just smiles . . .

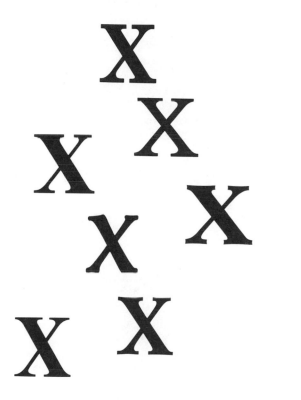

or blushes . . .

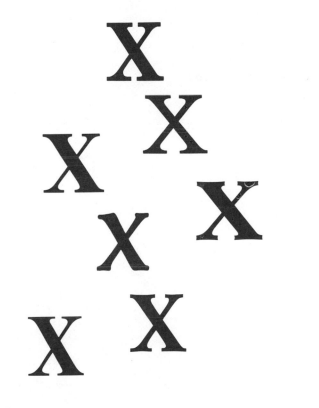

or fidgets uncomfortably . . .

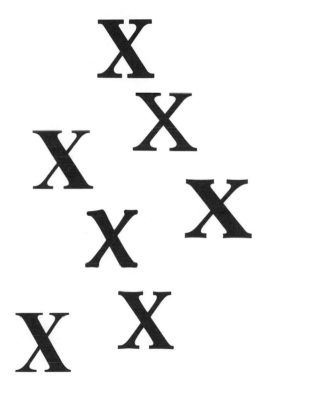

or just tries to ignore the whole thing.

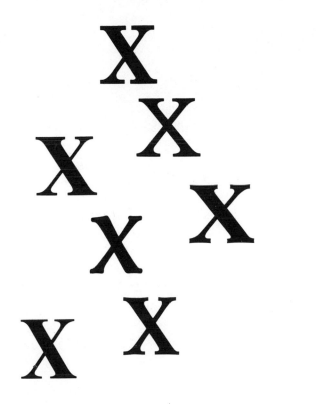

It doesn't take much of this to make the O feel like just an observer of the X's, an outsider who learns to be quiet at meetings.

But even if the O can still do its own job while it is isolated, being on the outside of the X group is not good for the O's career,

 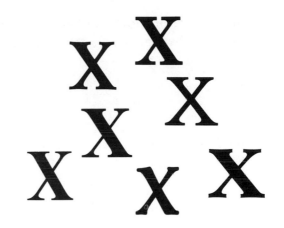

because, as we all know, the "old-X network" is very
important in helping people get ahead in any
organization.

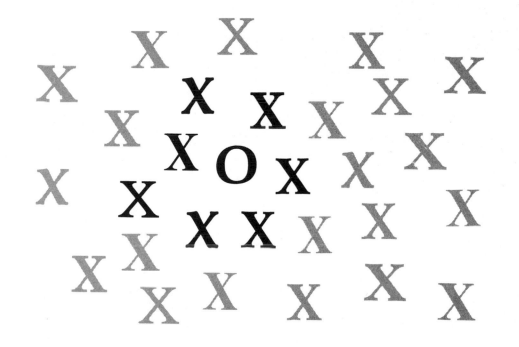

And whereas all the X's have lots of other X's behind them—

    to sponsor them,
      support them,
        recommend and endorse them,
          speak up for them at meetings they can't attend,
            teach them the *real* tricks of the trade
              and back them up—

the O might have to stand completely alone. With no one to provide any of that help.

So the O does need, after all, to get into the X group somehow. How does it ever manage?

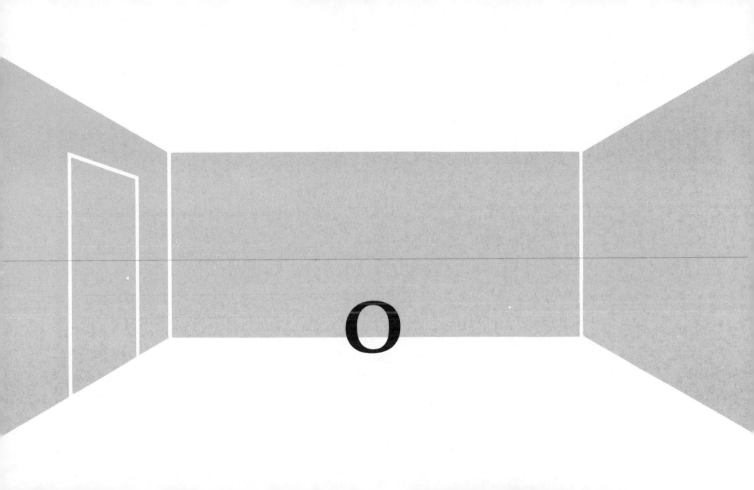

One way it gets in is by allowing the X's to define it as an "X-ceptional O."

"You're *not like all those other O's.*"
"You *think like an X.*"

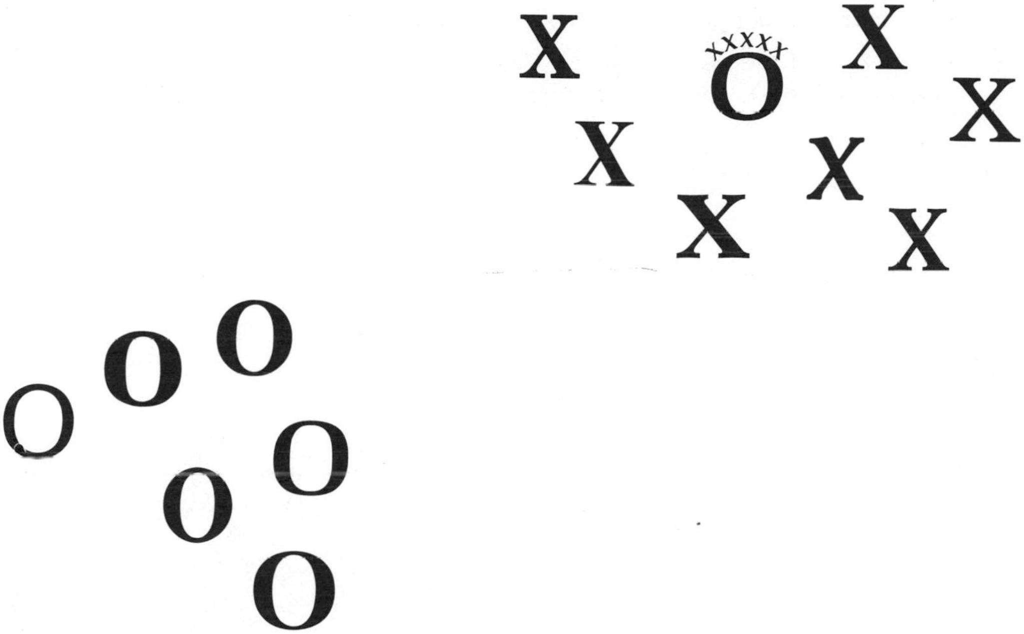
X
XXXXX
O
X
X
X
X
X
X
X
O
O
O
O
O
O
O

The O, of course, is supposed to show its gratitude to the X's for letting it in—by siding with the X's on issues of interest to O's, by adopting the X's point of view . . .

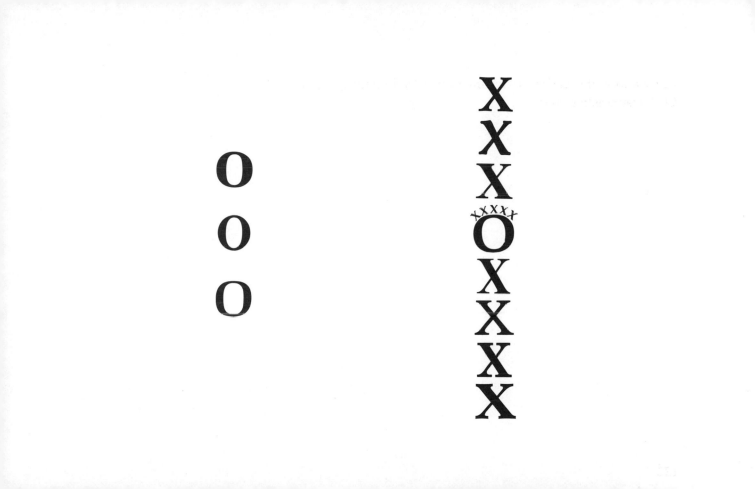

or by taking the lead in criticizing other O's, in putting down
O characteristics, and . . .

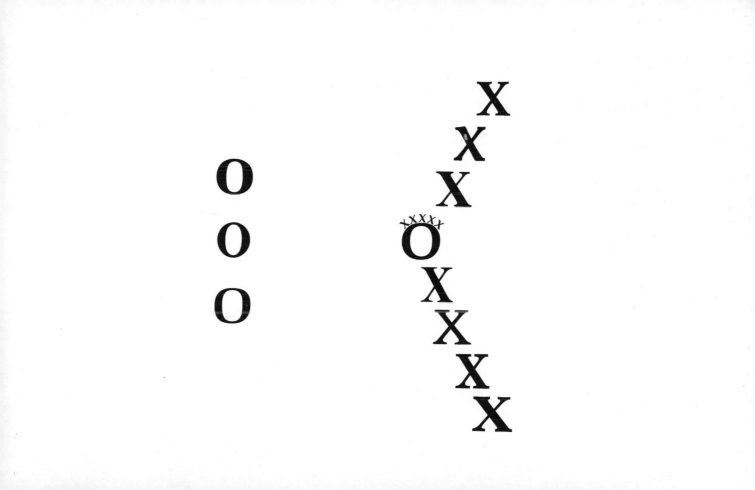

sometimes even in outdoing the X's in finding reasons to reject other O's.

All of which proves to the X's that they were right to let *this* O join their group.

"We sure picked a good one."
"That's our kind of O."
"Just like a regular X."

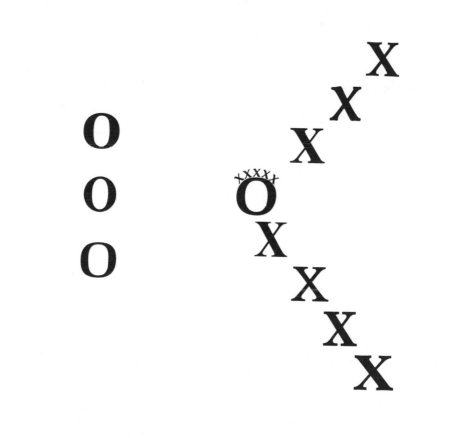

The O can also get into the X-group by developing a "good sense of humor." That means being willing to laugh at the jokes the X's might tell about O's.

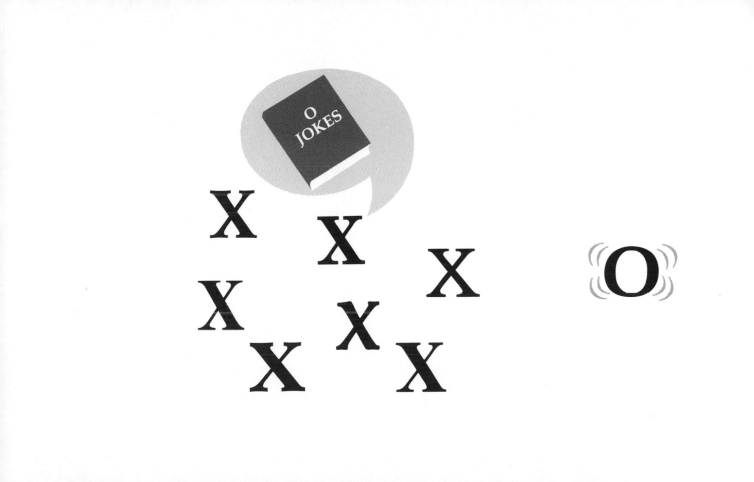

But of course the O doesn't dare tell any jokes about X's.

That would make them X-it fast.

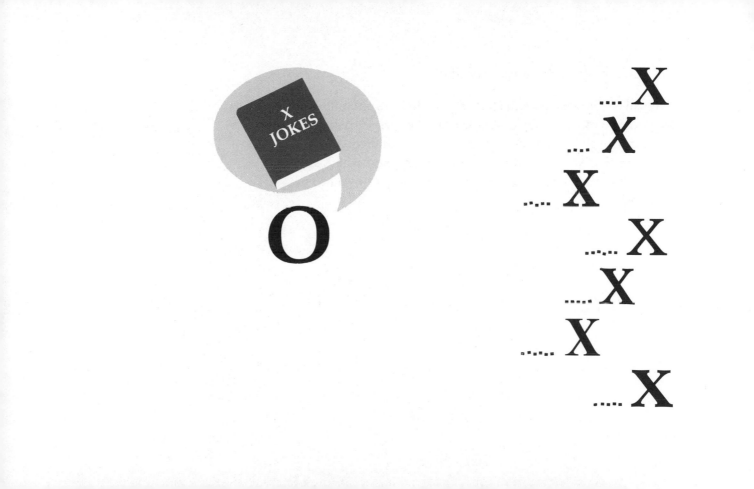

But don't think all this is easy for the O.

Even an X-ceptional O still feels torn sometimes and pulled toward other O's. Other O's make claims on the O, ask for contributions to O causes, invite it to side with them on issues, criticize and judge it for its behavior among the X's, and remind the O that it is still an O—no matter how "in" with the X's.

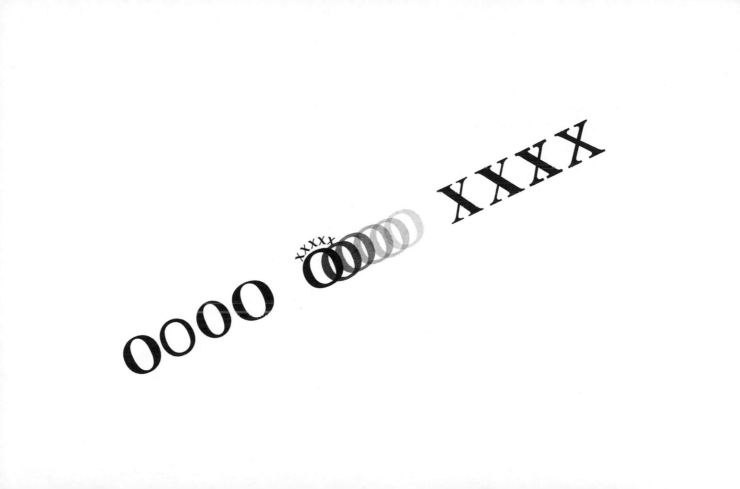

Nevertheless, the O might be pulled even more strongly toward the X's because it knows that in this place getting ahead depends on getting along with the X's one works with, and not on getting along with the other O's. In most organizations, "peer X-ceptance" is an important part of performance appraisals.

These pulls and tugs sometimes can make the O feel like a yO-yO.

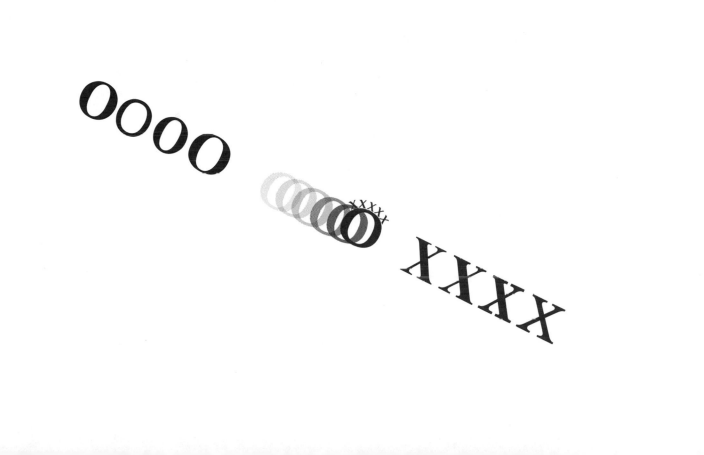

Siding with the X's leads to other popular conclusions about O's:

"O's are prejudiced against other O's."
"O's are their own worst enemies."

"We X's," they claim, "would really love to have more O's around here."

"But the O's," they say, *"can't seem to get it together. They are always tearing each other down."*

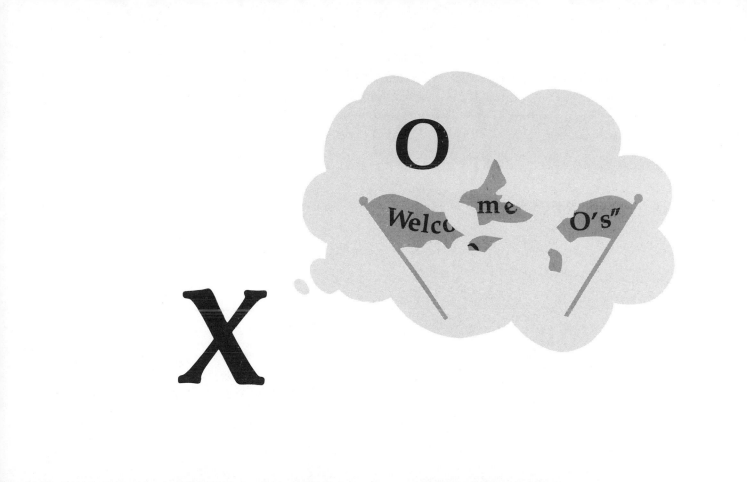

Of course the O's find it hard to "get it together." As long as there are so few of them among the X's, and as long as X's set the organizational standards, they do have to prove that they "think like X's."

X X X X X X X X X X X

X X X X X X X X X X X

X X X X X X O X X X X

X X O X X X X X X X X

X X X X X O X X X X X

X X X X X X X X X X X

Indeed, in this situation the O sometimes feels forced into competition with other O's, because . . .

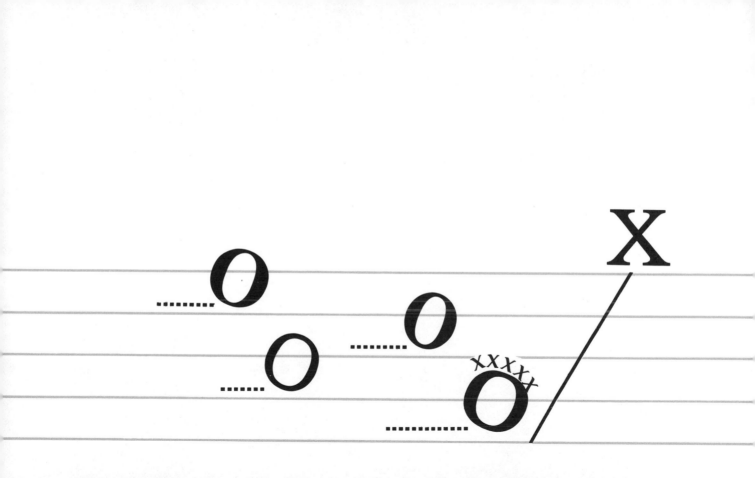

whereas all the X's see that X's have many places to move into,

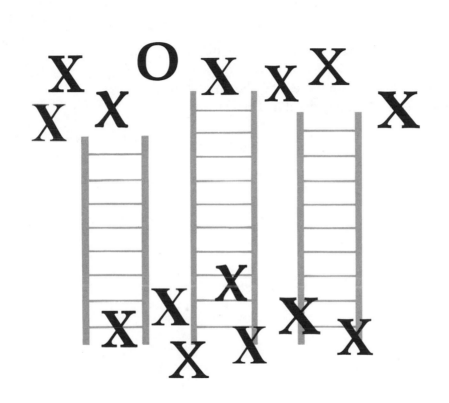

it looks to the O as though every other O around might be competing with it for its own hard-won place. That's one problem in having so few O's up there. The X's can support each other without even thinking about it. The O might have to go it alone.

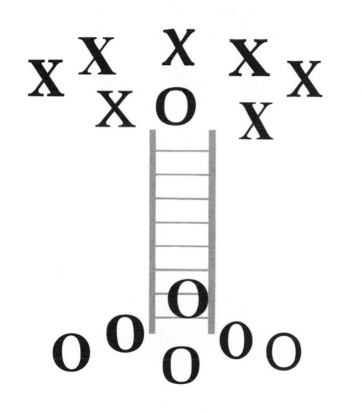

The third thing that happens to the only O in a group of X's is stere-O-typing.

It is much easier to stereotype the few than the many because there are too few examples around to contradict whatever ideas we have about O's in general. There are too few examples to show how different O's really are from one another—just as different, in fact, as X's.

Stereotypes

So we often engage in "statistical discrimination" by assuming that the *unusual* O—the one O among a group of X's—must be doing whatever the *usual* O does. Most of the time, we would be right. But we would be *wrong* for this particular O. This leads to a whole series of "mistaken identities"—where the O is assumed to be something it is not.

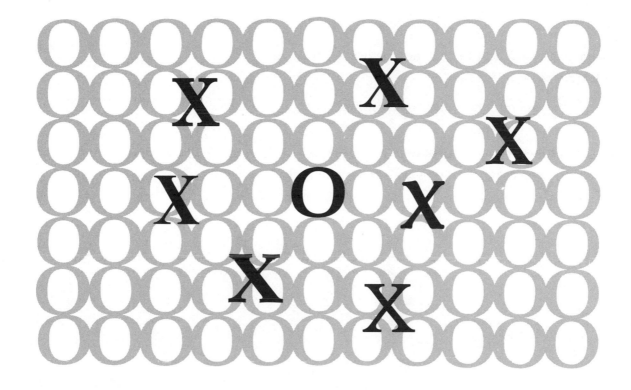

For example:

When you see an X and an O alone together, what do you think is going on?

What do you assume about their relationship?

Do you see them as equals?

Does one of them have higher status?

Do you see them as work colleagues—or something else?

Take another example.

When you see an O . . .

O

coming toward you . . .

on a dark street just outside the office late at night . . .

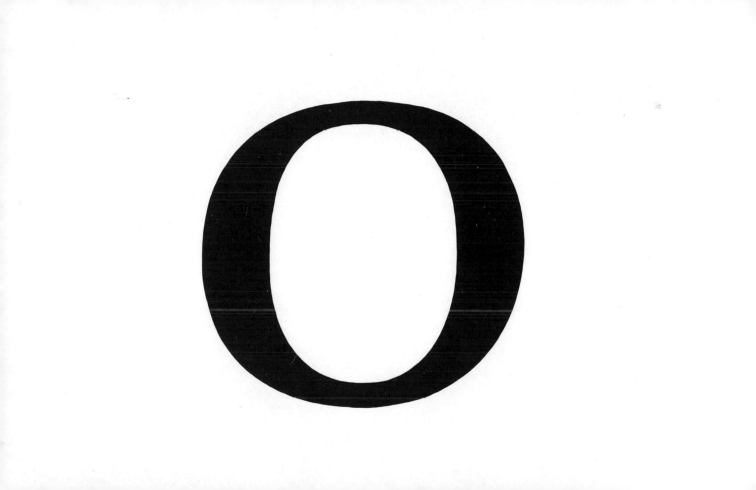

what thoughts go through your mind . . .

about what the O is doing there?

(But maybe the O was just working late?)

People also make different assumptions about O's and X's—even if they're doing the same thing.

For instance, it looks perfectly natural for a group of X's to be having a conversation around the water cooler, or over lunch.

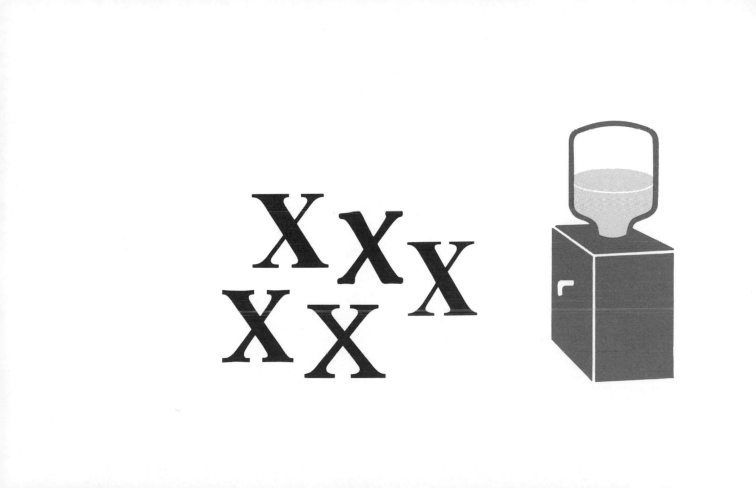

But when a group of O's does it, a different set of thoughts often passes through the X's heads.

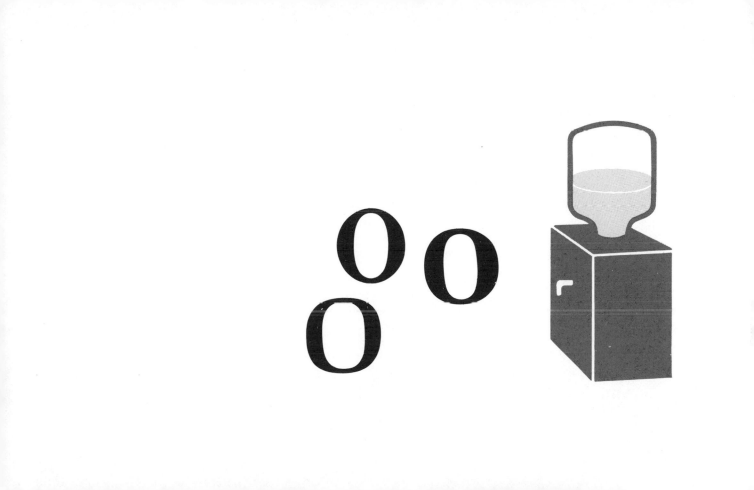

"Why are the O's suddenly getting together?"
"What are they plotting now?"
"It's some kind of a conspiracy."
"Let a few O's in and right away they want to take over."

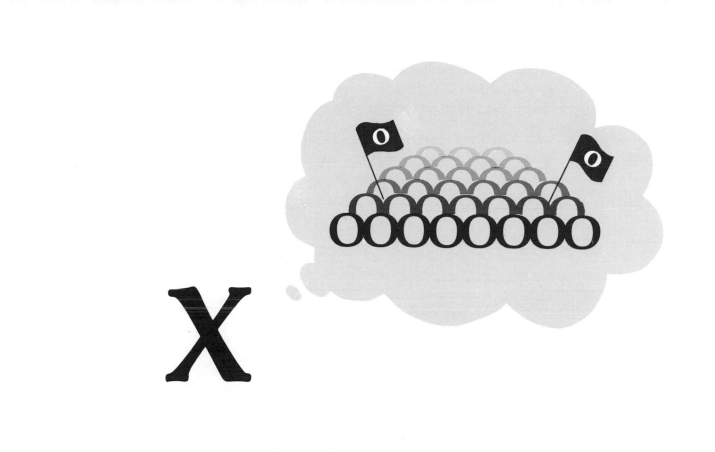

Organizations also reinforce stereotypes by deliberately creating O-slots: special jobs for O's, things that only O's are supposed to be good at, like taking care of other O's.

That tells the X's *why* there's an O in their group and keeps the O boxed in a special role. This further confirms the X's usual view of O's.

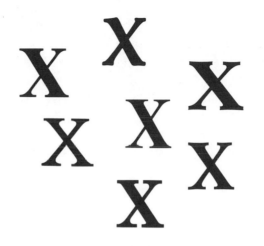

Informally, too, it is comfortable for both the X's and the O to fall into the old familiar ways in which X's have always treated O's, the traditional social patterns. The O sometimes colludes with the X's in these stereotypes because they make everyone more comfortable; no one has to change traditional behavior.

And it does give the O a special place, if a highly limited one, in the group.

There are four of these comfortable labels, and they're surprisingly universal. They are pasted on O's regardless of what it is that makes this O an O in that group of X's.

The first is:

Helper—

    servant

    support or caretaker

    "a good listener"

    "so understanding"

available to "give" to the X's and to do what they need done,
but clearly less important to the real business of the group.

The second is:

Sex Object—someone
   to be flirted with
   or fought over
   or admired and envied for (even imagined) sexual
prowess.

A seductress, an athlete or a stud. This happens especially to
physically attractive O's. But the attention they get has
nothing to do with business.

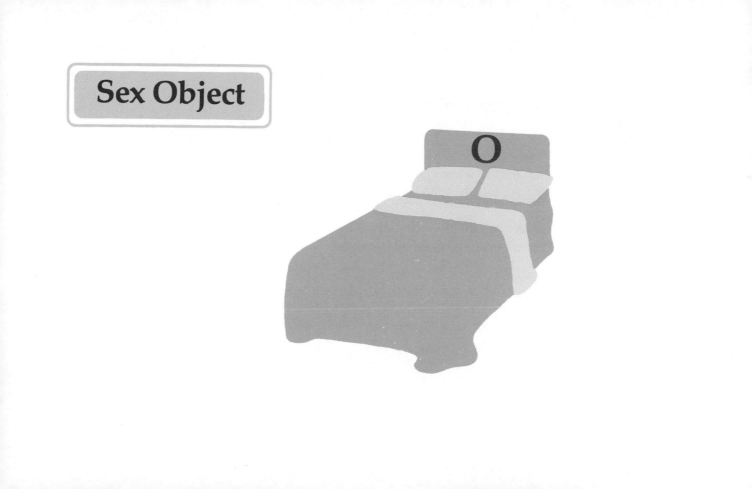

The third is:

Mascot—a nice role for young and lively O's—

    entertainer

    cheerleader

    lots of fun to be with *("terrific sense of humor")*

    comedian or song-and-dance O *("great rhythm")*

making the X's feel good as they go onto the playing field for the big game. This O cheers from the sidelines but never seems to get to play.

Mascot

Of course, these roles don't fit everyone. Some O's try to reject those three familiar stereotypes:

"I'm an individual. Treat me like one."

Well, there's a stereotype for that O too:

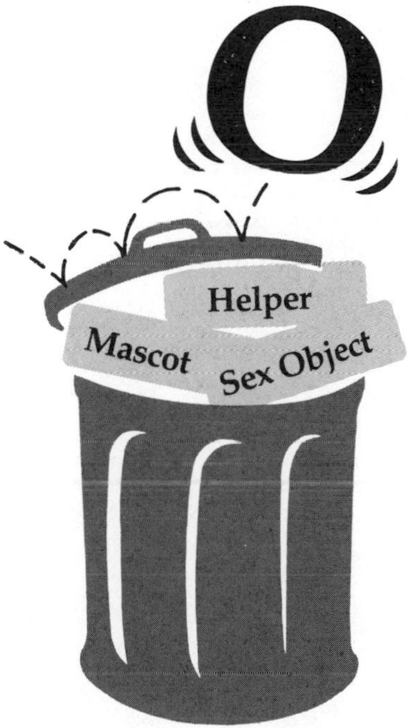
O
Helper
Mascot
Sex Object

Militant—

tough, dangerous
needs to be kept at a distance
"too aggressive"
"must be a radical"

This stereotype makes the O look tougher and more
dangerous than it really is and gives the X's an X-cuse to
leave it alone.

The problem with these labels is not just that they set the O apart from the X's. They are, after all, ways for the O to get along with the X's fairly comfortably.

Helper

Sex Object

Mascot

Militant

The problem is that none of them have anything to do with business. All of them take attention away from the O's competence and attach it to things that have nothing to do with the job.

There are also some special traps associated with these labels that make it hard for the O to be an equal member of the organization.

In the case of the first three stereotypes—Helper, Sex Object, Mascot—the X's are likely to engage in . . .

Helper	Personnel
Sex Object	Admin.
Mascot	Finance
Militant	Design

Overprotection.

They help the O even when it doesn't need it. They give the O an easier, safer job, protect it from risks, and don't give it any chance to demonstrate what it can do under fire. They do for the O things it can perfectly well manage by itself.

Since organizations reward risk-takers—or people who do the X-traordinary—the O is kept back, the O is kept powerless.

It can never show that it can do anything *but* the stereotyped tasks, and it does even those with too much help.

In contrast, the Militant O is threatened with . . .

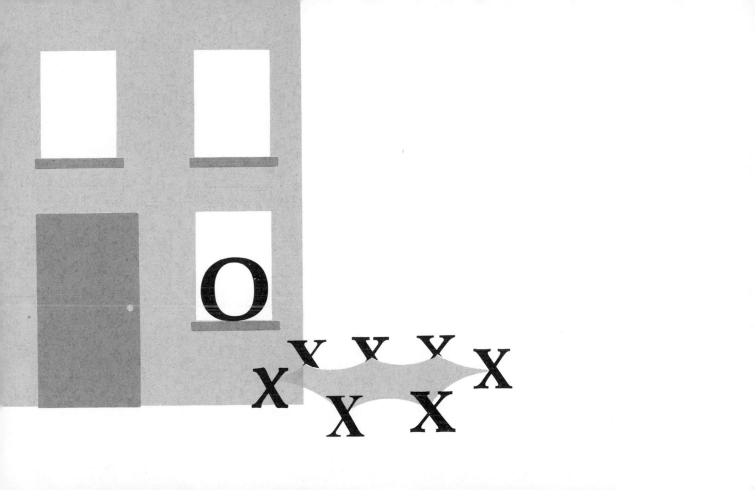

Over-X-posure.

The X's won't help this O even when it needs help. The O is given harder tests than the X's and more chances to fail.

"Sorry you're having trouble, but you didn't want preferential treatment."

If that O fails, as it often does, the X's feel that it's only what an "uppity O" deserves.

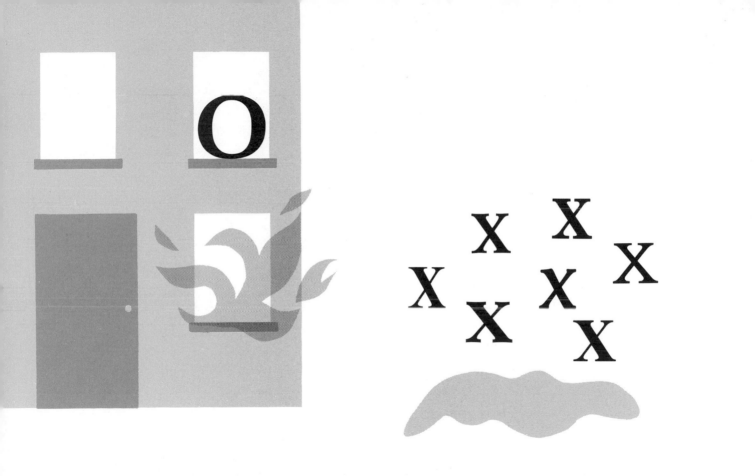

If one O in a group is subject to these pressures and stereotypes, does it help to have two O's? Are two O's enough?

X X O X X X X X X

Not really. Because then it's easy for the X's to see one as "our good O" and one as "our bad O." One gets all the flattery and attention, the other gets only criticisms and complaints. The two are set against one another. The "bad O" resents the "good O" for having it easy and for setting the standards. The "good O" knows that it had better not get too close to the "bad O" or offer any help, because it might lose the X's approval and support.

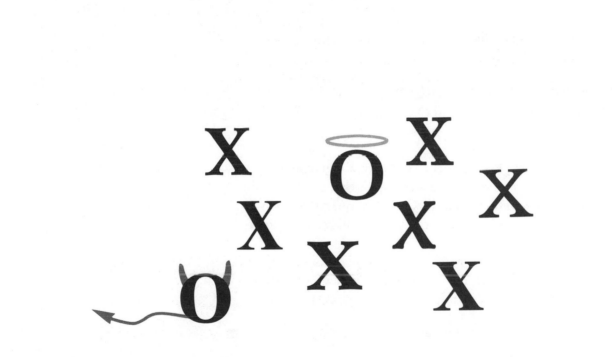

Or sometimes, when there are two O's, the X's think they've solved the problem of O-ness.

"Those two can take care of each other."
"We don't have to think about O's anymore."
"Now we've got things right. The O has a partner."

Of course, this can keep both O's isolated, away from the mainstream. And it never occurs to the X's that the O's might not *want* to be together, that the O's might not have much in common even though they're both O's. Do all X's want to be together?

These are some of the things that come up when there are so few O's in a group of X's. It doesn't make anyone very comfortable.

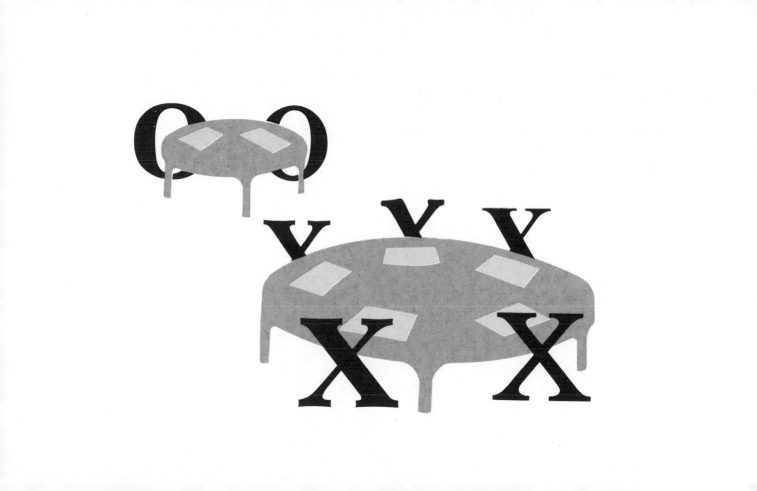

But just imagine how different a *A Tale of "O"* would be if the numbers of X's and O's were more balanced.

Look at this group. No one stands out as obviously unusual.

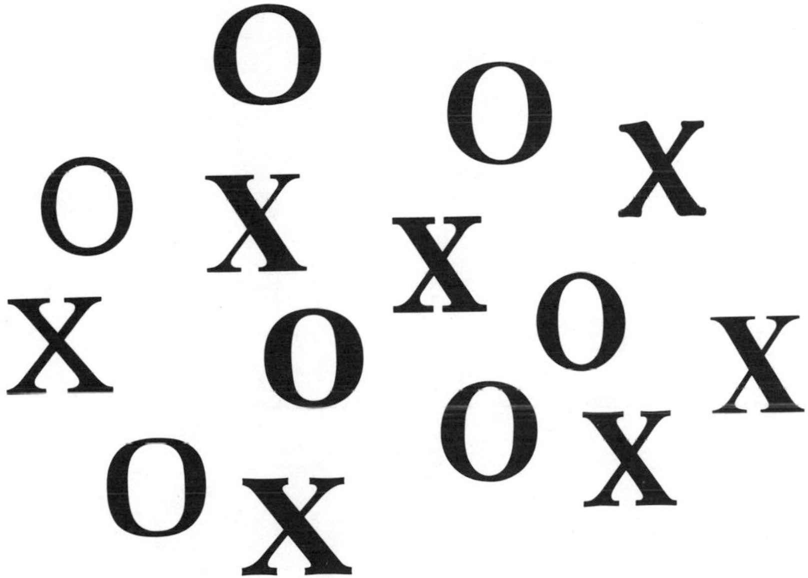

O
O X
O X X
X O O X
O X
O X

Everyone can be an individual. We can see that both X's and O's come in different varieties.

O X O O X O X O X O X O X X X O

And O's can work with other O's as well as with X's. The group can work together unself-consciously, and in many different ways.

That's why numbers count.

Numbers, of course, are not the whole story. Structures of opportunity—career ladders and who gets on them in the first place—and structures of power—access to resources and political support—also play an important role in the fate of O's and X's. But numbers do have impact.

X X X O X
O
O O
O
O X X O
X

The story of the X's and the O's is a good example of how the *position* shapes the person. That's why the drama is so familiar.

The O is forced to play a particular part because of the nature of the situation it is in—in this case, being one of very few of its kind among many of another kind. The O's choices are limited: it is forced to act in predictable ways. The super-star O willing to work twice as hard and the O who can stand back and laugh at it all do have an easier time. But all O's can benefit from building support systems—"the new O network"—that can reduce their isolation. And they can learn how to approach X's one on one. Simply understanding what happens in this situation can often help O's do better.

In real life, the O deserves a standing Ovation for managing a difficult role.

The X's, too, are playing out a part dictated by numbers. They are as much caught by the situation as the O's, acting according to a structural script. They need help in understanding some of their own behavior, as well as what happens to the O. When X's recognize the times that *they* have been an O, they can often be more sympathetic to the O's in their midst. And with more understanding, the X's can often see new options for acting. They can see why O's need support and why O's are sensitive to some remarks.

In the future, each X can be encouraged to play a different part.

Then we can close the curtain on *A Tale of "O."* With more O's given a real chance, with more O's able to cope effectively because they understand what's going on, with X's aware of their own behavior and its impact on the O's, and with both O's and X's seeing new insights and new options, we can all stop playing set parts and get back to our real work.

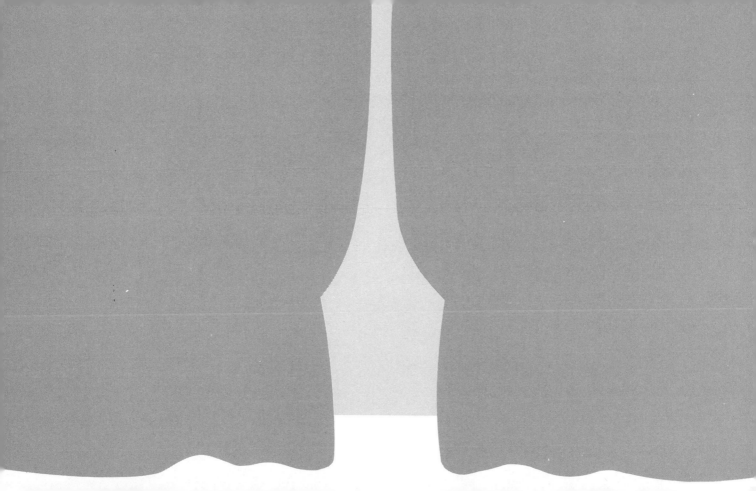

We can stop thinking of ourselves in categories like X or O
and see ourselves as just people—people who happen to
come in many . . .
different . . .
kinds.

A Tale of "O"

"X" RATED

A Serious Note

A Tale of "O" is an admittedly provocative title. Our purpose in choosing it was not only to be funny. We also want to suggest that prejudice can be obscene and that the impact of discriminatory treatment can be degrading.

We hope that once people recognize the universality of the X-O situations (practically all of us have been O's, even temporarily, at some time in our lives), new understanding and insight will lead to new options for individual behavior, for managing groups of diverse people, and for changes in organizations concerned with equal employment opportunity—with giving all kinds of people a fair chance to succeed.

A great deal of social science research supports the events and tendencies reflected in the story. Observations in large corporations (reported in Rosabeth Kanter's book *Men and Women of the Corporation*, especially Chapter 8) are confirmed by UCLA psychologist Shelley Taylor's laboratory experiments conducted at Harvard. These findings, as well as others, indicate that much of what happens to members of "outsider" groups when they join majority groups but are still few in numbers stems from their relative distinctiveness. Pressures and stereotypes tend to occur *regardless* of the special characteristic that makes the person an O. Of course, sometimes people are O's only briefly and temporarily: one doctor on a committee of lawyers studying medical malpractice policy; one man at a meeting of a women's club; the only non-native-language speaker in a group; a tourist in a foreign country. Sometimes the O characteristic does not dominate the person's entire life chances. But in many other cases—as currently with sex, race, cultural background or physical handicaps—people are likely to find themselves O's rather more of the time.

The story of the X's and the O's describes only what happens when people interact under conditions of unequal representation. It does not account for how the unequal numbers developed in the first place. For that, one needs to examine history and larger social structural forces, such as selection and tracking mechanisms. Numbers alone also do not explain how differences in status affect behavior or how positions that are nominally equal may hold unequal power. (For more information about these issues, see Chapters 6 and 7 of *Men and Women of the Corporation.)*

But when one wants to understand group dynamics in mixed groups, especially when there are newcomers, outsiders, strangers or "deviants," then the X-O metaphor becomes a very useful tool. It provides a new, less emotion-laden language, which blames neither the X's nor the O's for what occurs. It makes it possible for everyone to look to the *situation*—and not to the problems of specific individuals—as the source of any awkwardness that might arise or any difficulty the O might encounter. Now, sometimes individual problems *might* play a role (a somewhat incompetent O or a downright prejudiced X), but we have found that more often than not it is the X-O situation that creates trouble. The O simply does not have the same chance as the X's to show its competence, unless it is one of the unusually talented O's who can function well despite obstacles. Thus, one of the messages in this tale is that familiar findings about out-groups that blame individual member characteristics (they "fear success" or compete excessively or can only perform traditional roles) should be reinterpreted as stemming instead from stressful or competitive or stereotyped situations.

A Tale of "O" does not attempt to discuss the theory underlying each of its points: *why* X's and O's behave as they do. But the order of the tale follows exactly the order of the theory and research findings presented in scholarly form in *The American Journal of Sociology,* March 1977, and in *Men and Women of the Corporation.* Briefly, there are three theoretical rationales: (1) from *cognitive psychology,* holding that the fact of an object's distinctiveness heightens awareness of it, exaggerates the difference between it and the more common objects, and, if it is in an unusual place, induces perceivers to "force-fit" the distinctive object to pre-existing notions about its usual place; (2) from the *social psychology of group identity,* holding that groups form their boundaries in relation to deviants or outsiders and know themselves by contrast to what they are not, therefore needing to remind the outsider of its difference in order to remind group members of their similarity; and (3) concepts of *marginality in cross- cultural interaction,* which hold that strangers or newcomers make a group conscious of previously taken-for-granted norms, and that at the same time these cultural strangers may find themselves marginal to both their host group and their own cultural group—torn between two worlds. There are also references to "melting pot" theories of the process of cultural assimilation; in early stages of the entry of new people into a host culture, they may try to shed all vestiges of their own culture and deny any connection with it. Finally, some pieces of psychoanalytic theory apply here; for example, the tendency to polarize objects of anxiety into a "good" and a "bad" version.

There are universal social forms that tend to elicit universal responses. *A Tale of "O"* is about one of those forms: the awkwardness that is generated by transitional times in a pluralistic society, when a few people of one kind join a group of another kind.

X-O situations will never completely disappear. Even with respect to some obvious O's (by sex or race) it will be a long time before numbers are balanced in enough places that the O's in X-groups no longer seem unusual. What can O's and X's do in the meantime?

What O's Can Do

—Recognize the pressures of O-ness; find ways to relax and get away from pressures from time to time.

—Avoid unreasonable blame for difficulties; recognize the situation as a source of pressure.

—Talk with other O's about O-ness; share coping strategies and support.

—Develop the skills required to succeed in one's job; remember that competence is the "bottom line."

—Learn how to publicize one's skills and job competencies rather than one's differences.

—Carry or wear "recognition signs" that make it clear that one is there to do business.

—Search out opportunities to demonstrate competence, e.g., special projects, task forces, etc.

—Talk with X's, use them as learning resources; treat them as "experts" so they feel motivated to help.

—Offer resources or help to the X's so that X's need the O's.

—Develop diplomatic skills for handling/confronting awkward X-O interactions.

—Avoid making an issue out of every insult or tease; learn to let it roll off your back—or develop a good sense of humor.

—Seek opportunities to join in X networks so that these networks may serve both X's and O's.
—Seek out X's one by one to develop relationships, rather than always facing them as a group.
—Emphasize what the O has in common with some of the X's rather than what makes them different.
—Avoid overload from too much service as a representative; preserve energy for hard work at the job.

And, in Addition: What X's Can Do

—Increase awareness of what it means to be an X or an O and learn about X-O relationships
—Scrutinize one's own behavior towards O's:
   Whom do you consider suitable for what types of jobs or assignments?
   Who receives opportunities to get visibility?
   Who gets the training opportunities?
   Are there things you discuss with only some kinds of people?
      —Are any of these critical to success?
   Who receives how much of what types of attention (e.g., support, scrutiny, performance appraisal, advice)?
   Whom do you trust to do the important jobs?

—Provide opportunities for O's to work with other O's as well as with X's—but don't force the O's to be together if they don't want to be.
—Confront areas of discomfort (e.g., Can you tell an O that it isn't dressing properly? How do you relate to an O socially?)
—Consider what resources, skills, information people need to succeed and make sure that everyone has equal access to these things.
—Help O's get into the X-network.
—Pair O's with old-hand X's so that O's can learn appropriate behavior and tricks-of-the-trade.
—Be sensitive to how O's might feel about some of the X's jokes or conversation.
—Recognize that O's come in many different kinds; avoid stereotypes.
—Avoid over-protecting or over-testing O's; give them a fair chance to meet challenges.

Research Background and Further Reading

America, Richard F., and Anderson, Bernard E. "Black Men at Work: Must Black Executives Be Superstars?" *The Wharton Magazine*, Vol. 3 (Spring 1979): 44–47.

America, Richard F., and Anderson, Bernard E. *Moving Ahead: Black Managers in American Business.* New York: McGraw-Hill, 1979.

Campbell, Donald T. "Stereotypes and the Perception of Group Differences." *American Psychologist*, Vol. 22 (1967): 817–829.

Coser, Rose Laub. "Laughter Among Colleagues: A Study of the Social Functions of Humor among the Staff of a Mental Hospital." *Psychiatry*, Vol. 23 (1960): 81–95.

Dentler, Robert A., and Erikson, Kai T. "The Functions of Deviance in Groups." *Social Problems*, Vol. 7 (1959): 98–107.

Epstein, Cynthia Fuchs. *Woman's Place: Options and Limits in Professional Careers.* Berkeley: University of California Press, 1970.

Fernandez, John P. *Black Managers in White Corporations.* New York: Wiley, 1975.

Hughes, Everett. "Dilemmas and Contradictions of Status." *American Journal of Sociology*, Vol. 50 (1944): 353–359. Also in *Men and Their Work*. Glencoe, Ill.: Free Press, 1958. (About Blacks in White groups.)

Kanter, Rosabeth Moss. *Men and Women of the Corporation.* New York: Basic Books, 1977.

Kanter, Rosabeth Moss. "Some Effects of Proportions on Group Life: Skewed Sex Ratios and Responses to Token Women." *American Journal of Sociology*, Vol. 82 (March 1977): 965–990.

Kanter, R. M., and Stein, Barry A. *Life in Organizations.* New York: Basic Books, 1979. Chapters on "The Gender Pioneers" and "The Managers."

Laws, Judith Long. "The Psychology of Tokenism: An Analysis." *Sex Roles*, 1 (1975): 51–67.

Sarason, Seymour. "Jewishness, Blackness, and the Nature-Nurture Controvery." *American Psychologist*, Vol. 28 (November 1973): 962–971.

Schreiber, Carol Tropp. *Changing Places: Men and Women in Transitional Occupations.* Cambridge, Mass.: M.I.T. Press, 1979.

Segal, Bernard E. "Male Nurses: A Study in Status Contradiction and Prestige Loss." *Social Forces*, Vol. 41 (October 1962): 31–38.

Seifert, Kelvin. "Some Problems of Men in Child Care Center Work." Pp. 69–73 in *Men and Masculinity,* edited by J. H. Pleck and J. Sawyer. Englewood Cliffs, N.J.: Prentice-Hall, 1974.

Spangler, Eve; Gordon, Marsha; and Pipkin, Ronald. "Token Women: An Empirical Test of Kanter's Hypothesis." *American Journal of Sociology,* Vol. 84 (July 1978): 160–170.

Taylor, Shelly, and Fiske, Susan T. "The Token in a Small Group: Research Findings and Theoretical Implications." In *Psychology and Politics, Collected Papers,* edited by J. Sweeney. New Haven: Yale University Press, 1979.

Taylor, Shelley E., et al. "The Categorical and Contextual Bases of Person Memory and Stereotyping." *Journal of Personality and Social Psychology,* Vol. 36 (1978): 778–793.

Wolman, Carol, and Frank, Hal. "The Solo Woman in a Professional Peer Group." *American Journal of Orthopsychiatry,* Vol. 45 (January 1975): 164–171.

Zaleznik, Abraham; Christensen, Charles R.; and Roethlisberger, F. J. *The Motivation, Productivity and Satisfaction of Workers.* Boston: Harvard Business School, 1958—sections on "Status Congruence" (about being non-Irish-American in an Irish-American work group).

A Tale of "O" is also available in full-color on videotape or slide-tape from Goodmeasure, 6 Channing Place, Cambridge, Massachusetts 02138.